YOUR KNOWLEDGE HAS VALUE

AF149666

- We will publish your bachelor's and master's thesis, essays and papers

- Your own eBook and book - sold worldwide in all relevant shops

- Earn money with each sale

Upload your text at www.GRIN.com
and publish for free

Alex Ngumbi

The impact and effect of project and change management approaches in delivering business change

GRIN Verlag

Bibliografische Information der Deutschen Nationalbibliothek:

Die Deutsche Bibliothek verzeichnet diese Publikation in der Deutschen National-
bibliografie; detaillierte bibliografische Daten sind im Internet über http://dnb.d-
nb.de/ abrufbar.

Imprint:

Copyright © 2012 GRIN Verlag GmbH
Druck und Bindung: Books on Demand GmbH, Norderstedt Germany
ISBN: 978-3-656-55487-5

This book at GRIN:

http://www.grin.com/en/e-book/265538/the-impact-and-effect-of-project-and-
change-management-approaches-in-delivering

GRIN - Your knowledge has value

Der GRIN Verlag publiziert seit 1998 wissenschaftliche Arbeiten von Studenten, Hochschullehrern und anderen Akademikern als eBook und gedrucktes Buch. Die Verlagswebsite www.grin.com ist die ideale Plattform zur Veröffentlichung von Hausarbeiten, Abschlussarbeiten, wissenschaftlichen Aufsätzen, Dissertationen und Fachbüchern.

Visit us on the internet:

http://www.grin.com/

http://www.facebook.com/grincom

http://www.twitter.com/grin_com

The impact and effect of project and change management approaches in delivering business change

Table of contents

1. Introduction

Change management is defined as a structured approach for transforming organizations, teams and individuals from their current position to a future state which is desired for fulfilling or implementing a strategy or vision. In simple terms it is a form of organizational process which aims at empowerment of employees for accepting as well as embracing changes taking place in their immediate environment.

This paper will specifically emphasize on issues related with leadership and management required for delivering business changes within the organization and in its workforce. Managing changes is associated with project management and is a distinct process altogether. A discussion based on the significance and ruling of the change agent has also been done. This is because the role played by the change agent is significant to trigger organizational changes and make them acceptable to the workforce. The chief difficulty faced by the agent is managing individual resistances against change. It is human nature to be resistant to change due to habit. The conflict lies in the interests of the manager and the client regarding a project which help in forming the challenge of leadership and empowerment and also serves as the point of debate for the change process. Since managing change in itself is a distinct process, it is important to discuss the competencies and strategies that need to be implemented (Anderson, 2010).

2. Organizational Change and Project Management Aspects

Today, the business world is reshuffling at a rapid pace. The worldwide market economy, aging population, technology developments and global competition are creating a long-lasting impact. Today, large number of workers disengages themselves when the company they work in does not do what is right and cannot manage the changes well. Whereas in companies where the employees believe their employer to be caring and honest in managing change finds only 40% of the employees going disengaged. The most critical driver for organizational productivity and effectiveness is employee engagement which is rapidly declining in the Northeastern companies since the last few years.

A study by Wallinger(2006) suggests that the principle on which the projects implemented by multiple organizations is based on is the need for innovation in the current business state. The British Standards Institution suggested that monitoring, controlling, planning and motivation are required in the management process of projects in order to achieve the project's objectives. It is asserted that every organization must fulfill its duty of defining the crucial elements of project management based on its business strategies and corporate structure (Wallinger, 2006).

The process of project implementation has both the strategy and structure of the organization being affected by innovation. This fact serves as a reference for project management as the key change agent and it also helps in considering it in a wider context rather than just the project's technical implementation. Project management is difficult as it comprises of taking decisions in context with innovating within an organization effectively (Anderson, 2010).

Bertocci (2009) stresses that change management is the renewal process for the capacities, structure and direction of the organizational characteristics in continuous manner to serve the rapidly changing consumer demands both externally and internally. It is asserted that the main objective of managing change is integrating the business processes, strategies and individuals along with the existing technologies. Executing such integration requires examination of the multiple management tools and techniques to be used in a practical sense (Bertocci, 2009).

3. Human Elements of Project management

Buckley (2013) asserts that it is not at all easy to implement a successful transformational or change strategy for bringing about organizational transformation because there are various work streams that need to be integrated successfully to bring about the desired change. It is true that the preparations done previously are quiet important but the actions which are taken while implementing the change and after the change has taken place is equally critical. Thus, it requires application of an integrated process for planning comprising of the steps to be taken before, after and during the process of change (Buckley, 2013).

It is believed that the key direct impact of project implementation is on the organizational business but the core and most important element which must be considered by change management is the people related to it. This is because launching of strategies, structures and organizational culture is carried out by individuals being the most important deciding factors for the success or failure of the project. The techniques, motivation and team building process are the key enabling factors for managing change along with the direction tools, controlling and correcting people's behavior with the aim of changing the present status of the organization (Sibbet, 2012).

Morris (2010) asserts that it is quite easy for an individual to do a task in the right manner all by themselves rather than motivating others to do the same task in the right manner. Change realization and product implementation are executed in both hostile settings and conflicting interests. Thus, it is safe to say that leadership is quite significant for implementing change successfully and depending on the human needs and movements of the different soft skill techniques. Today, the traditional idea of management being a collection of various technical skills offered by the notion of product leadership has shifted to the it being perceived as a significant attribute for communicating the visions and inspire people and make things move on the right direction to bring about the required change and manage it (Morris, 2010).

4. Business Change Techniques/Strategies and Change management agent Roles

According to Carter & Ulrich (2004) it is a consideration that a project is nothing but a technique to bring about change in an organization but in the practical sense much attention is paid to the real actions required for implementing change. However, change management plays a significant role in project management as it includes managing the impact created by the project deliverables. This impact is either indirectly or directly spread within the organization. This means that sustainable results are expected from a project but change management limited to the project's scope is not adequate (Carter & Ulrich, 2004).

The challenges associated with change occur during the project's life cycle and is usually not limited to a specific method of project management or does not involve referring to the technical failures. The main problem takes place because they are not considered as a core competent and important part of the project which needs management.

A study by NĂSTASE (2012) describes that the agent of change plays a significant role by fulfilling its responsibility of initiating the entire change process so as to guide the organization in dealing with the newly formed circumstances resulting from the project's progress. However, the agent of change has not yet been defined in specific terms. The change is triggered based on the context associated with the change. An agent of change is the one who is responsible for change of the status quo of the organization. The agent of change plays the role of mitigating confusions, boredom, laziness, anger and disenchantment along with organizational anxiety (NĂSTASE, 2012).

The role that must be played by the agent of change is usually played by multiple individuals during the project's life cycle. Authors suggest that during the project's beginning stage this specific role can be satisfied by a consultant also residing outside the organization. The efforts to bring about the change can be made during the project's initiation or maturity with the help of the implementation team comprising of the organizational employees. However, when the change process begins to face away, a management at a very high level of the organization must intervene to take up the role of the agent of change which seems to be the best solution that time. This solution is supported by Carter & Ulrich study which defined 4 distinct models proposed by some author being considered as the key agents of change reaching management, consultancy, team models and leadership (Carter & Ulrich, 2004).

In view of this approach, adaptation can be accomplished in a slow manner being implemented with the help of staged initiatives. Reconstruction results in faster realignment of the company operations. Evolution is defined as that for of transformation change which is well-planned and slowly implemented but is sure to be implemented. Generally a revolution is considered to be the most fundamental aspect of transformational change that is implemented within a short time period.

Five distinct focuses favoring change might exist within an organization known as identity, work ways, key relationships, mission and culture. In spite of this it can be said that these elements need change when any one of the lot experiences possible changes.

Two distinct approaches have been asserted favoring change which is carried out in a planned manner for the emerging change. However, it can also be argued that there are no practical, clarified and accepted approaches for managing organizational change which can explain the actual changes required by the organization along with the ways to incorporate them. Any project aiming at bringing about successful changes within the organization comprises of three distinct steps in order to undo the present level moving on the next level and then freezing it again. It is proposed that in order to successfully adapt the all new behavior it is important to guard the past behaviors and previous cultures and structures (Soriano, 2012).

According to Roberts (2013) the most established and effective approach for bringing successful change within an organization is to carry it out in a planned manner. However, since 1980, this approach has been widely criticized. It is suggested that the idea that this approach emphasized on changes which are both incremental and small-scale. It is not applicable in situations that need change which is rapid and transformational. On the other hand, it can be said that a planned approach is based on assumptions depending on which the organizational operations continue within the constant conditions. It is also known to have the ability to shift such that the one single aspect is stable when compared to other and is well-planned previously. Thus, the planned approach towards change becomes unaware of the situations in which directive based approaches are required (Roberts, 2013).

This planned approach has widely been criticized for organizational change which has motivated the emergence of another approach. The emergent approach does not visualize change to taken place from the top to bottom but visualizes change which is from the bottom to the top. This approach suggests that the change is so rapid that the senior managers find it impossible to identify and plan effectively and also finds difficult to implement the expected organizational responses. This result in making the organization's responsibility to bring about change to be less involved.

It is believed that the emergent approach comprises of the ongoing accommodations along with the alterations and adaptations having the ability to bring about fundamental changes devoid of prior intentions of doing so. In the author's words, the emergent approach of change occurs when the routines are re-accomplished and when breakdowns are being dealt with and the routine opportunities and contingencies associated with work. Bulk changes go unnoticed as small alterations get lumped into a big collection making the required noise (Wallinger, 2006).

It is also stated that there are no universal rules for managing and leading change. Supporters of the emergent approach towards change suggest the entire action sequence to be followed by the organization. However, multiple suggestions which have been mentioned here are likely to be abstract and turn out to be difficult to apply. There are authors offering practical guidance for the managers and organizers.

Change is the need of the hour and this requirement had never been so intense. This is because the present world is evolving continuously within a competitive business environment. Successful management of change has skewed results being largely endeavored to possess within the repertoire. It must be noted that organizational management of change is presently non-systematic, non-continuous and reactive. The failure rate of all the change programs that have been initiated is as high as 70%. Based on the problems mentioned above, it is adequate to give a good definition for describing agent of change in the form of the core element of Human Resource management during the project implementation process (Gans, 2011).

5. Leadership in bringing about business changes

According to Smillie (2001) one of the likely queries related to significance of managing change and related difficulties that might occur is to identify the one who is the most suitable candidate within the organization to play the role of the agent of change to assist others and implement the entire transformation process within the organization (Smillie, 2001). There are a number of factors that need to be considered such as the conflicts existing between the project manager and owner which prove to be the constraint for the process of change management. It is also important to consider the disadvantages and advantages related with agents bringing about internal change (Soriano, 2012).

The Principal agent theory is the main theory based on which the relationship between the project client and manager is framed. It is suggested that all problems associated with this concept is likely to be structured as the problems and adverse selection of moral hazards. It must also be mentioned that the issue of mistrust occurs when the project client and the manager influencing low interest of the project giving a false perception about progress and lack of a comfort zone (Sibbet, 2012).

6. Roadblocks of Organizational Change management

Each and every change initiative aims at introducing novelty within the organization's current state. Thus, it is important for people to learn about brands and novel ways to perform new and challenging tasks. The main reasons for people to be resistant to change can be the various years comprising of uncertainties or it can be called habit also. Resistance is defined as the most significant factor which determines if the change initiative will be a failure or a success. Sometimes resistance results in unexpected expenses delaying the entire process of strategic changes. In other words, resistance towards change aims at maintaining status quo where there are pressures for altering it (Smillie, 2001).

The complicated and modern approach to change favors resistance. In this context, resistance to change is considered as a phenomenon which is influenced by multiple factors which are irrational, political, and rational and management factors. It is usually not under the guidance of a dis-satisfied individual. Resistance can also be considered as the driving force or energy for the organization. Thus, the best way to deal with resistance is to convert it and utilize it rather than eliminating or avoiding it.

The most important and primary step is to comprehend the different forms of resistance that are available in the beginning in order to consider the most suitable method which can help in dealing with change. Resistance usually occurs at 3 distinct levels known as the organizational level, individual level and the group level. Organizational level resistance is linked with power and conflicts when profits and benefits are the results of change for one part of the organization and harmful to other parts of it (Soriano, 2012).

7. Recommendations

In order for a change process to be effective it cannot be termed to be an afterthought. It is a fact that it needs a comprehensive attempt comprising of all organizational levels driven from top to bottom. Change has now become a constant in the modern world but it requires a focused orchestration and planning to become a success. This discussion highlights the need for change when a project is implemented (Anderson, 2010). It is suggested that management of change must be considered as a distinct process having a unique identity in context with project management. It is the job of the change agent to address the approaches involved in context with the nature of the organization and the changes which need implementation. An organization requires an agile workforce which can respond effectively and perform as well as adapt to the rapidly changing demands. This is very important for the organization to thrive and be successful in today's tumultuous and rapid-paced markets (Sims, 2002).

This can be done by following a number of well-established steps. Firstly, it is important to develop the plan with well-defined goals. The second step is to identify as well as develop effective behaviors for managing change in the organization's workforce focusing them on the organization's future plans and purposes. The third step is the careful implementation of the process which comprises of leadership support, strategic communication, success measures and development. This approach enlists the employees by making sure that they realize what they are doing, what are their capabilities and they know well the reasons for doing so. Following these steps can help an organization's workforce to be agile so as to fulfill the changing demands with their change initiative. It will also help the workforce to perform at levels which make sure that the company stays competitive and fulfills the strategic goals even in times of tough competition and rapidly changing economy (Carter & Ulrich, 2004).

Success must be defined right at the beginning along with the metrics used for assessing the achievement of the objectives and goals. For instance, sometimes it is important to measure the abilities of a manager in order to communicate effectively with some employee regarding the emerging change. In such situations, it is suitable to ask for direct reports which can be evaluated for the interactions that took place. On the other hand, when success is considered as the way in which the organization manages change, then the employees can be asked to fill up opinion surveys prior to and after taking the change initiative

8. Conclusion

This discussion highlights the need for change when a project is implemented. It is suggested that management of change must be considered as a distinct process having a unique identity in context with project management. It is the job of the change agent to address the approaches involved in context with the nature of the organization and the changes which need implementation. Promoting trust and understanding with the project manager and client will bring about a positive impact on resistance management to trigger change within the organization.

Managing changes is associated with project management and is a distinct process altogether. A discussion based on the significance and ruling of the change agent has also been done. This is because the role played by the change agent is significant to trigger organizational changes and make them acceptable to the workforce. The chief difficulty faced by the agent is managing individual resistances against change. It is human nature to be resistant to change due to habit. The conflict lies in the interests of the manager and the client regarding a project which help in forming the challenge of leadership and empowerment and also serves as the point of debate for the change process. Since managing change in itself is a distinct process, it is important to discuss the competencies and strategies that need to be implemented. It is critical to highlight the main areas where the employees will be affected. It can be a system for managing new performances, mergers or reorganizing an existing team and then the suitable communication tools need to be implemented to guide them in adapting the changes. The metrics that are used can also be restructured so as to reinforce specific behaviors.

9. References

Anderson, D. (2010). *Beyond Change Management: How to Achieve Breakthrough Results Through Conscious Change Leadership.* LONDON: John Wiley & Sons.

Bertocci, D. (2009). *Leadership in Organizations: There is a Difference Between Leaders and Managers.* New york: University Press of America.

Buckley, P. (2013). *Change with Confidence: Answers to the 50 Biggest Questions that Keep Change Leaders Up at Night.* london: John Wiley & Sons,.

Burnes, B. (2013). *Organizational Change, Leadership and Ethics: Leading Organizations Towards Sustainability.* london: Routledge.

Carter, L., & Ulrich, D. (2004). *Best Practices in Leadership Development and Organization Change: How the Best Companies Ensure Meaningful Change and Sustainable Leadership.* london: John Wiley & Sons,.

Gans, K. (2011). Should You Change Your Thinking about Change Management? *Strategic Finance; , 19,* 34-90.

Morris, P. (2010). *The Wiley Guide to Project Organization and Project Management Competencies.* london: SAGE.

NĂSTASE, M. (2012). The Impact of Change Management in Organizations - a Survey of Methods and Techniques for a Successful Change. *Review of International Comparative Management / Revista de Management Comparat International; ,* 5-16.

Roberts, P. (2013). *Guide to Project Management: Getting it right and achieving lasting benefit.* NEW YORK: SAGE.

Sibbet, D. (2012). *Visual Leaders: New Tools for Visioning, Management, and Organization Change.* london: John Wiley & Sons.

Sims, R. R. (2002). *Managing Organizational Behavior.* london: Quorum Books.

Smillie, I. (2001). *Managing for Change: Leadership, Strategy and Management in Asian Ngos.* Chicago: Earthscan.

Soriano, D. R. (2012). Change management in the entrepreneurial Latin-American organizations: an overview. *Journal of Organizational Change Management ,* 653-656.

Van de Ven, A. H. (2011). Breakdowns in Implementing Models of Organization Change. *Academy of Management Perspectives; ,* 58-74.

Wallinger, H. (2006). Transitions: Race, Culture, and the Dynamics of Change. *Volume 5 of American Studies in Austria , 11,* 12-188.